Keepsakes and Celebrations!

Much to
Joy
your
Kathy !

Ginny

Keepsakes and Celebrations!

A Potpourri of Poetry

Virginia Pease Ewersen

VANTAGE PRESS
New York

FIRST EDITION

Copyright © 1997 by Virginia Pease Ewersen

Published by Vantage Press, Inc.
516 West 34th Street, New York, New York 10001

Manufactured in the United States of America
ISBN: 0-533-12352-6

Library of Congress Catalog Card No.: 97-90287

0 9 8 7 6 5 4 3 2 1

To the National Library of Poetry and all who have
encouraged me!

From my heart to yours.

—the Author

Contents

Keepsakes and Celebrations!

A Pineapple Welcome!

I counted my pineapples today.
"Now what kind of wealth is that?" you say. . . .
It's the richness of mem'ry of the Clipper Ships' Day!
When the counting is over, I'll tell you more . . .
Three are stencilled on my bright front door,
One on a sign in the entryway.
Two are in windowpanes, catching the light,
Six more on the walls of my kitchen white!

"Cap'n John is home, today!"
A pineapple speared on his white picket gate
Meant, "I'm HOME! What a happy Fate!"
After sailing a year through tropical seas
And seeing so much he could hardly believe,
He hung out the fruit so his friends would perceive:
"You're WELCOME! I'll share the tales of my peregrine
    days
On the seas and in ports, where I've LIVED many
    WAYS!"

Dayspring!

I don't like to miss the morning,
I love the Earth before the "world" begins. . . .

I test old sayings. . . .
Does rain before seven REALLY stop before eleven?
Usually. (I've been there to know.)
Does the early bird REALLY catch the worm?
Yes. (When the ground is damp, but firm.)

I listen and watch. . . .
On the road, the neighbor's cat aims for home,
Anxious for breakfast and a good day's rest.
From the north, a cheerful rooster crows!
At dawn, the birds sing in celestial chorus!
The sky reflects the glory of the unrisen sun!

I LOVE the EARTH before the "world" begins!
I DARE NOT MISS THE MORNING!

Hope—from the East!

A solid row of trees is lined
Against the sky just blushed with rose. . . .
Their form is of a different kind—
Strong, yet top-edged in lacy rows. . . .
Centered above is VENUS, the bright and Morning
  Star—
In HOPE that LOVE will finally win
O'er the world's affairs as they are!

My heart and eyes behold this sight
As I seek the morning paper,
(Blithely tossed in a deliv'ry caper!)
To start the day, it's a beautiful rite. . . .
For my hopes are ever given more LIGHT!

Vane Wisdom!

The weather vane was still,
Pointing south as the sun arose!
The sky was a glorious, brilliant rose,
The Earth was azalea-suffused!
"Red sky in the morning, sailors take warning!"
All day people talked of the sunrise cerise,
Expecting lowering, lead-colored skies!
(The vane turned a bit to the east.)
But the day was a joy, the sky azure!
(The vane turned a bit more.)
At eve, the full Moon rose,
The world was awesome, blue-white aglow!
Next morn, the sky was blushing, again,
Still without a sign of rain!
(The vane turned more to the east.)
The clouds moved in!
The vane twirled and settled at "E,"
The rain poured, making the fields a tiny sea! . . .
OFTEN, life's signs are almost hidden,
But the vane is always turning to the time of action!
LOOK AT NATURE TO SEE THE REFLECTION
OF ALL OTHER LIFE, EVER SEEKING
COMPLETION!

The Catalpa Tree

Have you ever known a Catalpa tree?
One of the prettiest and stateliest you'll ever see!
Its leaves, large green hearts,
With flower trumpets of white
(With a bit of purple, placed just right!)
And, oh, their fragrance is so sweet—
The loveliest of trees I've chanced to meet!
I know, for one stood in my childhood yard. . . .
The cats and the hens let down their guard
And frolicked in the Catalpa's shade—
And <u>WE</u> pretended 'twas a forest glade!

Some Country ABCs

A is for Apples, red, yellow, and green
With flavors as varied as the colors they preen.
B for red Barns, old and too rare!
C for Clotheslines, "alive" in the breeze,
And for Curtains of white at windows bright!
D for graniteware Dishes as blue as the sky!
E for brown Eggs, fresh from the nest—
If you've ever tasted, you know they're the best!
F is for Fun while hard work's being done,
And for good country Food when day is done!
G is for Gardens—for food and beauty—
In the country, more pleasure than duty!
H is for Hayfields, like a sea of green!
I is for Indian relics unearthed by the plow,
Proudly displayed on tables low!
J for Joy at the rising sun,
And at end of day for work well done!
K for the King of the lawn, the blue jay—
Darting and flashing toward kitties at play!
L for sweet, brown Lanes that are worn through the
    farm,
Bordered with wildflowers, and "alive" with charm!
M for the mighty Machines that till and plant the soil,
In hope that all beings may have food more royal!
N is for Nuts, *a priori* of squirrels in Fall!
O for Old things made by skilled spirits, departed,
Still cherished or used as their grace is imparted!
P for Pastures, with one cow or many!
Q for Quilts, art sewn with great love!
R for wild Roses in erstwhile fence rows,
Edging the fields as June comes to a close!
S for the Songbirds as they nest in Spring,

Inspiring the people to whistle and sing!
T for a Turtle who DARES cross the road.
(He knows on the other side is a ditch!)
U for Upstairs with aerial view so rich!
V is for Vanes, foretelling the weather!
W for Wagons of Wheat, golden in the summer heat!
X for the "unknown" in each country day!
Y for Young animals ever close to the earth!
Z for the Zany, of which there's no dearth!
IN THE COUNTRY, IT'S EASIER TO LAUGH AND TO
    PRAY!
'Tis a GIFT to LIVE the ABCs of the country way!

April Astonishment!

The hyacinths are purple,
Their fragrance a delight!
A robin is a-singing. . . .
Out there, it's April-showering . . .
Oh, NO! It's April-SNOWING!
Chilly, downy puffs of white
Drift to emerald Earth and melt . . .
Such a whimsical, lovely sight
Had not yet set my eyes alight! . . .
NOR HAD MY SPIRIT FELT!

The Promise of May!

There is only one MAY in the twelve-month year—
So emerald and open and freshly dear!
The weeds have not started,
The flowers are "perfection,"
Young creatures frisk, hop, or go on the lope!
Birds are heard from every direction—
Their nest songs resounding with Joy and Hope!
When Winter seems long, and the clouds are gray,
It's lovely to think of the PROMISE of MAY!

Midsummer Reflections!

The light is incredibly bright!
The daytime wonderf'lly long . . .
The robin sings at peep of light
A melodious, throaty song!
The busy morning seems so fleet . . .
At noon, the flowers are extra sweet! . . .
Shimm'ring hours offer spirited peace . . .
(Which all wholehearted beings seek!) . . .
At dusk, the Robin trills again
To celebrate the day that's been!
Joyfully limned in his roundelay:
"TOMORROW IS ANOTHER DAY!"

Autumn Presaging . . .

Migrating Swallows lined the telephone wires . . .
Lilting Wrens were heard no more.
Fewer Robins pulled worms from mires!
Yet, bright summer flowers were still galore,
And the grass was still jade green!
Only a few Autumn signs were foretold:
The glow of the sun was more like gold . . .
The sky was bluer in the shorter day,
The stars like lanterns in the lengthening night.
At morning, there was a chilling mist—
Sudden gusts would drive it away!
THEN, the wind rustled the leaves with a rougher twist!
One day, a rosy maple leaf fell to the ground . . .
From then on, Fall signs did swiftly abound!

Luminescence!

'Twas a silvery gray and amber day—
Maize linden leaves were wafted down
On a soybean field of gold and brown . . .
The lemon sun shone through a veil of mist
And a single red hollyhock thus was kissed!
Was this an "ending" type of day?
OH, NO! For Tigey and her kitten tumbled at play!
Cats know that love is "Forever and Aye"—
So I petted them softly and went on my way!

Winter Alchemy!

The snow fell featherlike at night . . .
Then the Moon created a pristine sight!
The tardy Sun changed the snow to rose-white . . .
At noon, the Earth was diamond-bright!
As the short'ning day went toward twilight
The snow appeared to be opaline!

By the Moon, it was ermine, fit for a queen . . .
(But the snow showed many of the tracks of Life
By the time of the second icy night!)

Truly Sweet Memories!

The glossy oak case with sparkling plate glass
Held candies for all children's dreams!
Car'mels, Mary Janes, and Choc'late Drop Creams. . . .
There were Jelly Beans in pretty tones,
Each color had a flavor all its own!
Licorice Twists were the fav'rite of some . . .
Clove Drops were sharp on the tongue,
Rosy Fireballs made the tongue hum!
Circus Peanuts were banana-cream soft,
Horehound was even good for a cough!
Through the week, our pennies had to suffice!
(But we always held HOPE aloft!)
For the BEST of all times were Saturday nights
When Daddy bought a POUND of Rainbow Bites!

The Sheaf of Wheat!

Beautiful and graceful wheat—with amber plumes of
    grain
Has nourished and truly fed mankind
As centuries have waxed and waned!
When Man first found wheat, he chewed it
And found it good to eat . . .
He realized it could be food, along with his hunted meat!
To plant the wheat and harvest its seeds
Nomads forsook tents for pride-of-place!
They boiled it as gruel, and rejoiced in its taste!
Then, the Egyptians discovered yeast!
(What wisdom from the Middle East!)
Ground wheat, with yeast, produced a dough,
They baked it, and mankind had BREAD!
The Greeks put a wheat crown on Ceres' head!
In heraldry, the sheaf appeared on crests.
The "breaking of bread" offers cheerful rests!
As we travel about the earth—
Of the sheaf symbol, there is no dearth!
One often sees it, and it brings to mind
The importance of wheat to all Mankind!
HOWEVER (A POSTSCRIPT):
IF one asks for bread, give not a Heart of stone,
For "Man does not live by bread, alone!"

The Hen's Nest

Many years ago a little black-haired girl
Watched her father sawing wood
Into shapes that set her thoughts a-twirl!
"What is it, Papa?" she asked,
(When she had waited as long as she could.)
"Maybe it's a hen's nest, dear," he replied,
So, she went to play "dollies" even as she sighed. . . .
On Christmas morning, she found the "hen's nest"! . . .
In a beautiful cradle her "dollies" did rest! . . .
Today, that cradle graces my front room,
On it carved, "Dec. 25, 1904."
Above it, a picture of my Mother, that year—
Wonderful gifts from days of yore!
Mementoes of LOVE and Christmas cheer!
What's given in Love from a Christmas heart—
To other hearts is ever more dear!

The Golden Bouquet

The sun shone brightly on his hair!
A sweet smile brightened his eyes!
"Mommy, here are some flowers for you!"
He handed me the dandelions
He'd carefully picked from the dew. . . .
As I took the bouquet from his little fist,
A honey bee stung him on the wrist!
"Fix it, Mommy!" he cried.
I "fixed" the place with soda paste . . .
Soon again, his eyes were dried . . .
He was singing a little song . . .
Although I knew it could not be,
I silently prayed, "May he not have to bear
Stings that cannot be 'fixed'!
He's so loving and bright and dear!"
He's been hard stung in the years betwixt—
The tears took longer to dry . . .
But his being is REAL and STRONG!
He gives to others his WHOLEHEARTED SONG!
(And he wastes little time asking, "WHY?")
But I still get a catch in my throat, today
When I think of Dale, the bee, and the golden bouquet!

Joey—Intrepid and Eternal

Joey was a little striped cat,
The son of Wild and Tame!
The heart of a lion royally dwelt
Within his tiny frame!

At first, some cruel kids found him
As they plundered through the wood. . . .
Three ladies and a vet saved him from them;
He trusted humans who were good!

His bobtail was his half-mast flag,
His eyes a wondrous green!
In Fall, he'd hide beneath the leaves
Where he could not be seen!

His leaping, pouncing skills were great—
HIS SPIRIT SO SERENE!
(And on his grave, within a week,
The catnip sprang up green!)

Glorious Affirmation!

June 1934 . . . I can see and hear her, yet . . .
Singing, "Leaning on the Everlasting Arms,"
As she bounced my little brother on her knee. . . .
Two hours later, my ashen-faced uncle came in,
"Mother is GONE!"
(He found her where she'd been tending her beloved
     hens.)
Part of MY heart died, too . . .

June 1994 . . . All these years I've thought of
     Grandma . . .
When I was a child, and had a cut, she'd smile and say,
"It'll get well before you're married twice!"
(That was very good advice!) . . . TODAY, I opened her
     trunk! . . .
Jewel upon jewel—ten colorful quilts with stitches so
     fine!
She had put them so neatly away!

Grandma is NOT really gone! . . .
MY HEART IS RESTORED . . . THE EVERLASTING
     ARMS ARE REAL!

Floral Recollections!

Today, my daughter found a place to go
Where the Buttercups and Sweet Flags grow!
As we walked together along the trail—
Wildflowers of yore my mind saw, again . . .
Nature's loveliest treats ever viewed by man!
Trillium, Sweet William, and Crowfoot frail
Graced the old fence rows . . .
(Never touched by my uncle's plows!)
In the woods, (with Jack-in-the-Pulpit presiding,)
Buttercups, Violets, Bluebells, and 'Mallows
With Dutchman's Breeches danced in the light!
(A rainbow of purples, pink, yellow, and white!)
The carpet was emerald, the tree-curtains light green,
The sky the bluest that has ever been seen! . . .
In my mem'ry my uncle TOWERS!
(He whose plows never scathed the flowers.)
Indeed, he taught their names to me,
But he SHOWED me MORE—HOW TO HAPPILY
    "SEE"!

Zion Canyon, Utah, in July!

The splendor and majesty of Zion can never be truly
    described,
For the Creator on this land his own Hand has
    inscribed!
Its magnificence fills the soul with awe . . .
God built a "layer cake" three thousand feet high
Red on the bottom—white toward the blue, BLUE Sky!
Sometimes the buttes are sandstone-red,
Again, the red is crimson and the cones a purple-rose!
The golden sun on the aspens along the Virgin River
Mutates the reds as the shadows change—
There seems no limit to their range!
Now, look at the layer above—a-glowing, pristine white
Also reflected in the changing light!
The warm, soft wind rushes through the canyon
In a most rare, yet peaceful abandon! . . .
Seeing Zion, an experience sublime
Never dimming with the passing of time!
The treasure of mem'ry always keeps it bright,
My mind sees again The Great White Throne
Where the rocks are so steep it cannot be reached!
ZION IN ITS RADIANT, SPLENDID, MAJESTIC
    MIGHT!

With Much Gratitude . . .

In traffic, to make a left turn
Just causes my psyche to churn! . . .
But when I see the "Left" turn arrow,
I am BOLD and no longer like Jello!
So thanks to Traffic Control engineers—
Who have done so much to allay my fears!

The Windchime Messenger

Sometimes the universe seems inert!
The world seems totally unaware! . . .
Then, a melody brief and sweet
Is wafted on the silent air!
'Tis then one knows that God is there
At all times—both dark and fair!
Gossamer, celestial, surprising Joy—
A gift to the Heart—without alloy!

The Present

I like to bring the outdoors in
With windows bright and curtains thin!
When I work or write by my kitchen table,
I love to see out as much as I'm able!
The Earth changes as the seasons go:
Winter shapes in white are muffled.
Then, Spring comes with the trees green-ruffled!
Summer is bright and gay in full measure!
In Fall, the woods are a gold and red treasure! . . .
Before Winter again puts the Earth to bed . . .
So, in each of Life's Seasons it's good to vow
That it's always time to be pleasant!
And the best time of all is NOW!
"Look well to this DAY!"
It's a Gift called the PRESENT!

Spectrum Analysis

A rainbow's an awesome, ethereal sight—
It perfectly divides the light!
Red, orange, yellow, and green
With blue, indigo, and violet . . .
ALL ARRANGED IN A FORM INVIOLATE!
ABSOLUTES are hard to find—
The Iris reflects the MASTERMIND!

Of Butterflies and Hummingbirds!

Such delicate beings with strength of iron
To even survive in their earthly realm!
Their colors are bright as the flowers they love,
Their motions like a dream from Above!
Their size is SO small in the SCHEME of Things,
They're among the most fragile of creatures on wings!
Except for wings humming, the birds sing no sound,
Butterflies are mute, even though they abound!
They touch one's heart and imagination
With continuing Hope for Life's situation!

Mon Ami!

He's been my friend
When my world seemed to end!
He knows what to say to brighten my day!
To think of his laugh
Is a pleasure, indeed!
HE HAS AN AIR OF ACCEPTANCE
THAT MORE PEOPLE NEED!
True friendship cannot be defined—
It has too many facets
In each person's mind!
It's truly a Gift, which comes without measure . . .
A most pleasant, mysterious Treasure!

Herbal Grace Notes!

I savor my herb garden as I savor my life,
Each plant has a meaning all its own . . .
Named and described by ancient humans,
Each has a fragrance that truly illumines!
Their forms and hues show a very great difference—
Giving a variegated, tranquil appearance.
Each herb is useful in several ways . . .
When they're crumpled or touched,
Their aromas are wafted all ways . . .
This, to me, is like life's varied days!
Herbs are like grace notes, in peace and in strife . . .
The fragrance of lavender in morning dew
Is sure to lighten one's heart anew!
The salty scent of thyme will courage renew,
As did sky blue borage in olden times.
Pennyroyal sends insects to other climes . . .
Sweet woodruff, vanilla-piquant—
Is of butterflies a favorite haunt!
Delicious basil, the French say, "Herbe Royale."
There's catnip, by which the cats are enthralled!
Savory, with pretty white flowers,
Bees are ever close to its bowers!
Sage for longevity and balm for calm.
Camphorlike hyssop mentioned in Psalm!
These are only a few of the herbs in my garden . . .
Such life-enhancement is hard to imagine!
We must yet speak of rosemary . . .
For remembrance of many a friendly face!
Then rue, which the Greeks called the "Herb of Grace,"
They said that rue set the Spirit free,
Which it does, with its leaves of teal blue "lace"!

Helianthus!
(In Memory of My Father)

The sunflower brightens wherever it grows,
And turns to the sun as the daytime goes. . . .
This gracious flower, as the red sun sets,
Has seen so much it kindly forgets. . . .
And after it dries, birds feast on its seeds—
Positive proof that it does what it needs!
AND—a sturdy stalk, with a cheerful face
Is a MARVELOUS thing in the HUMAN RACE!

Heart Wisdom

"We'll slip the geraniums, today!"
My dark-eyed mother called to me.
I loved those words coming from her lips!
So to the creek we'd wend our way
To get the sand to set the slips!
We cut the slips so carefully,
And set each in a pot of sand.
My Mother worked so cheerfully
And words of wisdom gave to me!
"Just don't let dirt get in the heart,
Or the slips won't root and start . . ."
In Winter, the flowers graced the kitchen sills, rosy red!
    . . .

Now, I ponder the words my Mother said,
Geraniums and people have the same heart need,
'Twould be a grave error not to heed!

"Here is a boy with five small barley loaves and two small fish, but how far will they go among so many?"
—John 6:9

I believe that everything we say and do matters. Nothing we give is too small for God to use — a boy's lunch of loaves and fishes, a thoughtful word, a tiny act of kindness. The next time you are tempted to think that your small deed is of little consequence, remember: In God's hands it is like the proverbial pebble tossed into the pond. Its ripples may travel much farther than you might ever expect. *—Sue Monk Kidd*

Excerpted with permission from *Daily Guideposts*, 1983. Copyright © 1982 by Guideposts, Carmel, N.Y. 10512.

220-5748

Heart and Hand!

Twenty thousand years ago . . .
Hearts were carved on cavemen's walls!
Eons have passed, seemingly slow . . .
(Yet this lovely symbol never palls!)
For awhile, it was related to Mother Earth
Which, each Spring, has delightful rebirth!
Perhaps ancient ones saw redbud trees
With their heart-shaped leaves so rife!
All peoples have deemed it the center of life,
The soul and spirit of man—
From that, it led to veneration for God—
The beliefs of religions to span!
"As a man thinks in his heart, so is he."
Truer words there will never be!
Along with the hand reached out to befriend,
The heart bespeaks hope and life without end!

Compensation for Error

We were tooling down the freeway,
A sign said, "Turnpike, one-half mile."
But I thought, "That doesn't seem right.
I guess I'll stay in this lane, awhile."
Soon there were sights I'd ne'er before seen,
(Had I only heeded that sign of green!)

My trip home took me twice as long,
But I saw sheep in pastures, heard bird song,
And wildflowers were making meadows bright!
It's usually best to heed Life's signs,
(For sooner or later, it'll take more time!
But when one errs, the sweeter the flowers!
Though it uses up a few more hours!)

Counterpoint Days!

We often use music to describe life's days!
The days with "blue notes," which we call sad
Are evened by "grace notes," which we call glad!
Some days are "in tune" and some are "discordant."
On good days we're "high-pitched," on mixed days more
    "mordent."
On low days we're "flat," and on high days we're "sharp"!
On best days, we're in "chorus" melodious,
Earth seems "in tune," like a heavenly harp
That echoes its "score" harmonious!
Through these "counterpoint" tunes one can plainly see
It's "sweet" to "sing" Life in a "Major Key"!

A Merry Heart Does Good . . .

Sometimes it's hard to "keep" a smile
When the picture-taker says, "Hold it!"
Then he fiddles with the camera, awhile!
So, in Life, it can seem a trial
To maintain a smile
When the Master Planner says, "Hold it!"
But it's good to go through the motions,
(NEVER DENYING YOUR "NOTIONS") . . .
One day, you'll feel more cheerful emotions!
And though it's been many a weary mile,
You REALLY have not run out of SMILE!

Yesterday—a Parable?

"It'll not rain, now . . .
The garden'll never grow!
That blue looks painted in the sky!
The ground is hard with cracks SO wide!"

Hopelessness was heard on ev'ry side.
Low, frilly cirrus clouds drifted away . . .
(Which often mean rain could come, today!)
They appeared, but were wafted away . . .

At sunset, the wind rose and thrashed!
The sky darkened, the lightning flashed!
The thunder crashed and rolled!
Welcome rain came teeming, so bold!

Now, I am thinking of yesterday's morning—
How the cloud "seers" melted away . . .
The Earth is emerald again, today!
The Sun is gold in a sky of azure! . . .

Did the Planner of Days do this to ensure
That Man might more HOPEFULLY see and hear?
After all, GOD'S BEEN IN HIS HEAVEN
FOR MANY A YEAR!

Transcendent Compensations!

"Thank you, God, for milk and bread,
And OTHER THINGS SO GOOD!"
The children always said this Grace
Before we ate our food. . . .
Since, though I've tasted many a meal,
Their words into my spirit steal . . .
As I partake of the Menu of Life—
In famine, trial, and feast—
I've found those "OTHER THINGS" still RIFE! . . .
The lesser good the least!

Sensory Impressions!

Man must toil to copy the features
Of the natural senses of other creatures . . .
It took many minds to develop Sonar,
But a Fennec Fox can hear a beetle twitch across a
    field—
The Fennec, by Man, would be called a loner—
But to its true senses it will always yield. . . .
We try to sing to emulate
The birds who carol melodious trills!
Man is also weak in true listening skills
Even though his hearing is given high rate!
He must learn to be more aware,
To listen better, to really care!
To learn from Nature and her cosmic features!
Other creatures depend on SENSE for survival,
Man dares not stray too far from the Ways PRIMEVAL!

"Life-Light" Navigation!

When navigating in darkness
With the stars the only light,
'Tis a joy when the mirror of sunrise
Promises to be bright!
Then, when the Sun has arisen,
Look to the treetops for light!
When the ground path is more illumined,
Look ahead, not to left or right . . .
The shadow will be behind you!
Keep only the Wisdom you've learned—
Of Hope you'll not have lost sight!
(It truly pays to "travel light"!)

Repair? Reconstruction?

In all the history of civilization
Downfall has come to many a nation
From "the Cookie" crumbling on itself,
Beginning with EXCESS love of self!
This leads to greed and blindness to need!
Then respect is soon lost in a society
That had had a more kindly propriety!
No greater gift can a nation lose
Than that of good values and common sense!
The scheme is devoid of Light
When "Rights" count for more than "Right"!
The times have become so very tense,
Trust has gone by the way . . .
To ever restore the balance
Calls for patience and many to pray
For hope to improve each passing day . . .
That hearts will be changed
To a more kindly, truthful way,
That the twice-baked "Cookie" will be less deranged!

Reflecting on Choice!

'Tis good to slow wrath and to reflect
On what may SEEM a serious slight!
The pernicious violence of this Day
Stems from reflex action, with spite!
It's a constant choice each person must make—
Immediate reprisal or a truer survival!
Each decision, though seemingly small,
Produces peace or strife in the lives of all!
'Reflect' and 'reflex' only sound similar,
The world's Fate depends on these words familiar!
People need to go about "doing Good"
As is written of the Man who died on a rood!

Beauty and Truth!

There is beauty of Sound . . . and beauty of Light!
There's the beauty of Fragrance with its own elegance!
So graceful is the beauty of Flight! . . .
There can be real beauty in motion!
In all things around is beauty of Form!
(Beauty can't be defined by a simple norm!)
There's the beauty of Joys and TRUTHS newly found,
And the wonderful beauty of kindly notions! . . .
Sharing these with others is a Magic Potion!
It's a truly wondrous and winsome pleasure,
Which ripples and circles and echoes through time, . . .
Making "life's experience" uniquely sublime!

Surprises. . . .

When I thought my life was arranged,
By a phone call, Life's questions were changed . . .
The windmills keep turning, and I keep on learning . . .
From Life I will NOT be estranged!

There is no moral to my story
(Although my hair has grown hoary.)
But the strength that one gains, when hard fall the
    rains,
Keep blooming like Morning Glory!

A Peaceful Thought

Forgive me for any beings I've hurt,
Whether I knew or was not alert!
Then, the peace of soul I know
I'll share as far as MY heart can go!

An Outrageous Panorama!

Since the beginning of "Civilization,"
Goals have been set by the leaders of nations . . .
When the main goal is cruel exploitation,
Eventually, this turns to ruination
Of thought and individual being!
I think of the students in Tiananmen Square,
Their lives and dreams were just shot away!
(One can scarcely conceive of a darker day!)
For years, other beings have been destroyed—
Cruelty creates sorrow and a terrible void!
The children never have their chance . . .
How long can such a world advance?
How can presumptuous leaders DARE? . . .
In "The Realm of PROVIDENCE" is there a solution? . . .
Surely, there must be retribution!
True freedom of spirit will NEVER die! . . .
For this cruelty is based upon a LIE!

44

Babbling Semantics!

In ancient days, on Shinar's Plain
Men built a Tower called Babel . . .
There, many tongues were spoken, together . . .
They were sure they'd understand each other!
A wonderful world would be created—
All their needs would be magic'lly sated!
(The Tower fell—interpretations were in vain!)

Today, the whole world's a tower of babble!
So many languages—some standard, some created!
Men again are stressing communication! . . .
The Tower of Babel was destroyed—
The current babble leaves a great void!
Just when we think the Way is enlightened,
The misunderstandings are really heightened!
REMEMBER the misadventure of Babel!
(Is this reflected in the current timetable?)

Cosmic Glimpsing!

The trees are green and still . . .
Then, a flash of red,
A glint of gold,
A dart of purest blue!
A cardinal preens his crested head!
A goldfinch gleams in beauty bold!
A bluejay lights in the birdbath cool!

Then back again from whence they came . . .
The trees are still green, but NOT the same—
A rustle here, a flutter there—
Where birds are abiding—each with great care!

My heart is amazed beyond all "say"!
It's COSMIC glimpsing on a dazzling June day!

Eternity Manifest!

A comet is really too ethereal
To be described in penned material!
The beauty of its body and tail
A marvelous creation entail!
One looks up with wide-open gaze
To see a nebulous sight that's fleeting . . .
(Like Life, it only seems stationary,
Though this fact might elude the unwary.)
Each Life traverses endless, circular climes . . .
The comet, too, shall reappear
On very far-distant days and times!
(On seeing, as often as possible, the Hale Bopp Comet, in
Spring 1997.)

My Personal Stonehenge: The Sunset Refrain . . .

The Sunset moves from left to right
Behind my woods as the year gains light! . . .
In Winter, a cherry sun is far to the left . . .
In Spring, it's carmine, midway of the chartreuse
    hedge . . .
Midsummer finds it rosy-warm to the right . . .
In Autumn, it's scarlet, at the middle once more . . .
Then again, azalea, beyond the bay shore . . .
Each year, it's left to right and back again . . .
My Personal Stonehenge—The Sunset Refrain!

Perceptual Mapping . . .

Beach sand once was cliff-rock forms—
But now it leaves frail imprint!
Bedrock prevails through sun and storm . . .
Seldom varying from its norm!

When the gauge of Life is showing, "Low,"
Trace THAT in mem'ry's sand!
When Life's gauge is reading, "Full,"
Etch THAT on bedrock land!

Each graphs a log of his own Life's trek,
And when it's time for a map re-check
Roadway mem'ry needs a positive spin . . .
Then, perception of HOPE won't fray too thin!

Pollination Wonder!

Daylight has barely shone . . .
The dew is cool on grass and stone,
The air is sweet with summer flowers—
The very silence is sublime
With the quality of an ethereal clime! . . .
THEN, clearly heard is a steady bass drone—
A firm black and yellow bumblebee
Delves blue delphinium towers!

The bumblebee starts work at early morn.
(It has a furry coat which keeps it warm.)
It spends its whole day in a wondrous way—
Gath'ring honey and nectar each summer hour . . .
Carrying pollen from flower to flower! . . .
Another WONDER of Nature's own,
So useful to Man—yet toiling alone!

Reflection and Recollection . . .

I looked DOWN and saw the sky, today!
In the flower bed, in purest ray
Glowed forget-me-nots in random array!
'Twas a microcosm of Earth and sky! . . .
Bright green leaves under flowers purest blue!
So does Earth 'neath the heavens lie . . .
What a lovely reflection in May! . . .
A counterpart of Orb and the sweet-by-and-by. . . .